AN OPEN LETTER TO THE RIGHT HONORABLE DAVID LLOYD GEORGE

First published 1917
This edition published by Lector House in 2024

ISBN: 978-93-6138-454-7
Edition copyright © 2024 by Lector House LLP
All rights reserved under the International Copyright Conventions.

Lector House LLP
Registered Office: H. No. 96, Block C, Tomar Colony,
Burari, Delhi – 110084, India
info@lectorhouse.com
www.lectorhouse.com

AN OPEN LETTER TO THE
RIGHT HONORABLE DAVID LLOYD GEORGE

LALA LAJPAT RAI

2024

LECTOR HOUSE
LECTOR HOUSE LLP

AN OPEN LETTER TO THE RIGHT HONORABLE DAVID LLOYD GEORGE

PRIME MINISTER OF GREAT BRITAIN

BY

LAJPAT RAI

An Open Letter to the Right Honorable David Lloyd George

Prime Minister of Great Britain

Sir: I am an Indian who has, by the fear of your Government in India been forced to seek refuge in the United States, at least for the period of the war. In 1907, when Lord Minto's Government decided to put into operation an obsolete Regulation of the East India Company (III of 1818) against me, in order to put me out of the way, for a while, without even the form of a trial, Lord Morley, the then Secretary of State for India, defending his action, gave me the highest testimonial as far as my private character was concerned. You must have heard that speech though it would be presumptuous to imagine that you remember it.

My Credentials

Even my worst enemies have not been able to point out anything in my life which would give any one even the shadow of a reason to say that, in my private life, I have not been as good and honorable a person as any British politician or diplomat or proconsul, is or has been or can be. My record as a wage-earner is as clean and as honorable as that of the best of

Britishers engaged in governing India.

Mr. H. W. Nevinson, than whom a more truthful and honorable publicist is not known in British life, has said in his work, "The New Spirit in India," that once when he told a high Anglo-Indian official that I was a good man held in great esteem by my countrymen, the latter remarked, that because I had a high character in private life, I was the more dangerous as an agitator.

I am reciting all this as evidence of my credentials to speak on behalf of my countrymen. Just now I am a mere exile. For the present, I cannot think of returning to India, unless in course of time I begin to feel that by running the risk of being hanged or imprisoned, I should be doing a greater service to my country, than by remaining outside. I am now in the fifty-third year of my life, out of which more than thirty-four were spent in the limelight of public gaze. I am a man of family with children and grandchildren and have had my share, however small, of the good things of the world. Political freedom for India has been a passion to me ever since I was a boy. However hard the life of an exile or a convict may be, I am prepared to risk everything in the cause of my country.

In the language of that prince of political exiles, Joseph Mazzini, the word "exile," is perhaps the most cursed in the dictionary of man. It dries up the springs of affection; it deprives its victims of the sweet babblings and lispings of his little ones with whom every man of age loves to beguile the evening of his days; it closes the avenues of all comfort that are associated with that sweet word home; it shuts the doors of heaven and makes life a continued agony, hanging on the slender thread of such pity and hospitality as one may receive from the generous and kind-hearted foreigner.

India compared with Great Britain

How can I ask you who have perhaps never left your country except for some pleasant trips on the Continent, to put yourself in my position, if possible, for a moment only, and imagine how I long to kiss the soil, with which are mixed the bones of my mother and other forbears; how I miss the loving embrace of my beloved father, the sweet, expectant, imploring eyes of my widowed daughter, the devoted look of my wife and the kindly affectionate hand-shake of good and devoted friends. Nor can you realize how an Indian loves his country. How can you, of dark, sombre, fog ridden and misty climes, who are born of a chill atmosphere, of treacherously changing weather, who count hours of sunshine and months of darkness and fog and rain and snow and sleet, enter into the feelings of one whose country is a perpetual sunshine, and where universal light reigns—a country where weather is neither treacherous nor continually and rapidly changing, where beautiful dawns, starry nights, moonlit fields, resplendent waters, snow-clad hills and joyous rivers constantly and unremittingly fill one's mind with the sublimity, grandeur and beauty of nature; where one needs no stimulants to make him feel lighter and happier. An Indian needs no alcohol to forget his troubles. He has only to go to the Himalaya, or to the banks of Ganga, Brahmputra, Sindh or their numerous tributaries by which the land is blessed and fertilized. Oh, no! It is impossible for you to understand how passionately an Indian loves his country. He would rather starve in India than be a ruler of men in a foreign climate. For him, India is the land of Gods—the *Deva Bhúmí* of his forefathers. It is the land of knowledge, of faith, of beatitude—the *Gnan Bhúmí*, the *Dharma Bhúmí* and the *Punni-Bhúmí* of the ancient Aryas. It is the land of the Vedas and of the heroes— the *Veda Bhúmí* and the *Vir Bhúmí* of his ancestors. Yes, to him, it is the land of lands, the only place where he wishes to live, and more so, where he wishes to die. For a Hindu to die anywhere but in India, is as if he had been damned to hell. He shudders at the idea. To him, it is unthinkable. You may call it foolish, unpractical, sentimental and unprogressive; but there it is—a mighty fact of life into which no foreigner can penetrate.

Every Englishman loves his country, its darkness, its fog, its sleet and rain nothwithstanding. Who does not love his country and who does not say:

> Home, kindred, friends and country—these
> Are ties with which we never part;
> From clime to clime, o'er land and seas,
> We bear them in our heart;
> But, oh! 'tis hard to feel resigned,
> When they must all be left behind! —J. MONTGOMERY.

If then, an Indian decides to be an exile, voluntarily and maybe for life, he only does so either under a grave sense of duty or of danger. The duty lies in speaking *the truth* about political conditions in India and the danger in being effectively prevented from doing so if he remains there. No Indian can speak the *whole truth* while in India. The criminal laws of your Government—your Penal and Criminal Codes, Seditious Meetings and Conspiracy Acts, and Press Laws, your tribunals presided over by your own people unaided by jurors—effectively gag his mouth.

All honor to those who, though they cannot speak the whole truth, yet keep the fire burning in India and do as much as considerations of policy and expediency permit. If they do not speak the *whole truth*, they have at least the consolation of being at home, in the heart of their family and surrounded by their dear ones. For a political exile, however, there is nothing else to do, unless he has to carry on a fight for his living also, in which case he will divide his time between the two, that of earning bread and crying for justice for his country. Happily I have been comparatively free from much anxiety about the first. The only justification for my condition of exile, then, is that I continue to speak the truth about conditions in India and draw the attention of the world to them.

But an additional reason has just been furnished to me by the morning papers of March 15, 1917. It is said that your agents in India have decided to raise a war loan of $500,000,000, equivalent to 1,500,000,000 Rupees of Indian money, and also, to make the floating of the loan easy, your Government has agreed to increase the duty on cotton imports by 4% *ad valorem*. This war loan, it is added, would be a *"free gift"* of India to Great Britain! A free gift of $500,000,000 by starving, poverty-stricken India, to rich, wealthy, mighty Great Britain! Could anything be more astounding, more absurd and more tyrannical. The news has stunned me. I know that David Lloyd George, the British war-lord of 1917, is not the same person who was the radical Chancellor of Exchequer in the Liberal Government from 1908 to 1914, and who did magnificent service to the British workingman by reducing his burdens and alleviating his condition. I have been told that the said David Lloyd George is dead and you, sir, are an entirely different person. The Lloyd George of 1914 could not possibly have done the thing which you, sir, in alliance with Curzons and Milners have just accomplished. The newspapers say you are the same person; only you have changed. If so, the change is not of opinion but of personality. Evidently the soul of the original David Lloyd George has left the body to make room for an altogether different soul. We Indians believe in the possibility of such a metamorphosis taking place even in the lifetime of the same body! The best part of the joke, however, in connection with the £100,000,000 transaction lies in the fact that you call it *a gift by India—a gift indeed*. A gift like those given by Belgium to Germany. Is it not so, Mr. George? You are a shrewd person, very well educated, clever in diplomacy, well versed in tricks of speech and a master in statecraft; but even you ought to know that this trick will not deceive any one—not even the Indians who have been so often deceived by your predecessors in business. By way of adding insult to injury, you profess to do *"an act of justice"* to India by consenting to an increase of 4% on the duty leviable on imports of cotton goods. You say it is necessary for the success of the war loan of $500,000,000; but do you think that the Indians are so devoid of knowledge of the ordinary rules of arithmetic as not to understand what this "hitting below the belt" means to them? Your additional duty would but bring only $5,000,000 or $6,000,000 to the Indian exchequer, if the imports of cotton do not undergo a decrease. Your Government in India estimates it at £1,000,000 sterling. The interest at 5½% amounts to $27,500,000. Your Government in India estimates an annual charge of £6,000,000 sterling. Where is the balance to come from except from the famished Indian *ryot*? Is that how you show your love for democracy, for the people at large, for the workingman? Your representatives in India and outside, are proclaiming to the world that India is the most lightly taxed country in the world, withholding the fact that the average income of an Indian is only £2 a year, of which he pays 7 shillings toward taxes. That was before the new taxes were imposed.

Your publicists circulate another lie, viz., that India pays no tribute, while they know that from 20 to 40 millions sterling are remitted to England every year, out of which only a portion represents interest on loans made to India for the building of railways which your countrymen have used in developing their trade, and the remainder is the profit you make out of India. Then you cite the figures of trade in support of your theory that India is prosperous under British rule, but you forget that that trade benefits your country more than it benefits India, if at all. We send you food and raw materials at cheapest prices, making ourselves liable to "famines." You pay us in articles of luxury, of flimsy value, at the highest prices. The balance of trade is always in your favor. We toil and sweat, and your countrymen enjoy the profit. All the paying industries, railways, tea, jute, half of the cotton industry, etc., are in the hands of your countrymen. Theirs are the insurance companies, banks, railways and ships that profit by their trade. The railway rates discriminate against native industries and internal trade. Your countrymen get the plum-pudding, while our people cannot have even two meals of the coarsest food every day. When there is famine, millions die. Of late, your "scientific" methods of famine relief have succeeded in controlling mortality figures in famine days. The method by which you do this is genuinely scientific. Most of the deaths are charged to epidemics and disease; no one notices, however, that the havoc caused by disease is due to lack of nourishment and consequent low vitality. God-fearing Englishmen have cried themselves hoarse over the situation. The misery of the Indian masses has been pictured by their powerful pens in pathetic and soul-stirring words, but you and your colleagues still continue to ignore what they have said. New methods are every day being invented to exploit us. New departments with fat salaries for Englishmen are being multiplied. The public debt is being piled up. While hundreds of millions are spent on railways, nothing has been done to develop local industries. The country is suffering from lack of capital (cash and credit). (See Sir D. M. Hamilton's article in the *Calcutta Review* for July, 1916.) Every honest inquirer who makes inquiries on the spot and does not depend on the reports of your officials, finds and reports that the condition of the masses is the most pitiable (see the article by Mr. Manohar Lal in the *Allahabad Economic Journal* for April, 1916, and also the paper by Mr. Patro, of Madras, read in a meeting presided over by the Governor of Madras). For the latest British testimony on the point, see an article on Indian Industrial Development by Mr. Moreland, C.S.I., C.I.E., in the *Quarterly Review* for April, 1917, in the course of which he remarks: "It is a matter of common knowledge that the standard of life in India is undesirably low; that while the masses of the people are provided with the bare necessities of life of a bare existence [Are they?—L. R.] they are in far too many cases badly housed and badly clothed, badly doctored and badly taught, often overworked and often underfed; and that the present income, even if it were equitably distributed, would not suffice to provide the population with even the most indispensable elements of a reasonable life."

A careful study of the Reports on Prices and Wages discloses that the real living wage in the case of the vast bulk of agricultural laborers has considerably diminished, and this in spite of the absurd conclusion of the Prices Commission appointed by your Government a few years ago. No one knows better than you, Mr. David Lloyd George, that big buildings in cities, mostly owned by foreign capitalists exploiting the country; big trade carried on by foreign exporters and importers; railway mileage and receipts of Government revenue do not mean prosperity. Even the importation of treasure secured by capitalists in payment for exports does not indicate better conditions of the masses. If the masses are so prosperous, as your officers say, why cannot you tax the people for purposes of education and sanitation? Why is the death rate so high (over 30 per thousand)? Why can't you force the local bodies to spend money on education and sanitation? Why do your finance ministers say that there is no room for further taxes? Most of your agents in India know the real condition of the people but they have to conceal it from the British public as well as the world, as that enables them and their kin to continue in the enjoyment of that power which means so much to them.

In reply, you might well ask, why then is India loyal? Why do the people put up with all this? Why don't they rebel? Because they have been emasculated, and emasculated so completely, that they are absolutely helpless against your organized brigandage. They are weak, ignorant and incompetent. Sixty-four years ago they were not so helpless. But now they are completely demoralized and penniless. Your system has ground them into dust. They cannot even protect themselves from wild beasts. You have completely disarmed them. No Indian can possess a firearm except under a license from your magistrates, which is only rarely granted. You have completely hypnotized them by your professions of disinterested liberalism and altruism. The truth has, after all, dawned on them that you are the worst harpies they ever have had and if they could they would overthrow you without a scruple. You know that you are safe in their helplessness. When the war came they deluded themselves with the hope that in your hour of need you might accord them a better treatment, but by this time they have found their mistake and have concluded that, just as a lion may die of sheer exhaustion when attacked by an enemy rather than willingly loosen his grip on his prey so long as there is breath in his body, so a nation holding another in subjection might endanger her own existence without loosening her grip on her victim.

When the war broke out in August, 1914, I, with other Indian publicists, thought that however badly you had treated us in the past we had nothing to gain by German victory and the best thing, under the circumstances, was for us to stand by you and establish our claim to better treatment. The Princes and people of India therefore stood by you. You and your colleagues have been singing their praises and extolling their loyalty, but nothing has been done so far to give them even the elementary political rights of a free people. Verily, we have had a deluge of fine words but not an iota of deeds. On the other hand, you have imposed fresh burdens on us. While doing an "act of justice" about the cotton duties you have committed a wrong which wipes away the little good that might otherwise have been expected to accrue therefrom. Your courts and officers in India have taken away what little freedom the people enjoyed before. In cases of alleged sedition the sentences inflicted have been quite on a par with the doings of the Romanoffs in Russia. This time even women have felt your steel.

You knew as well as anyone else does, how the German government has been trying to win the good will of the Indians. It cannot be denied that the temptation was alluring. If, then, we have withstood it, it was not because we were in love with your Government in India, but on different grounds. Personally, I do not believe that any liberty is worth having which we cannot win ourselves, because liberty won by the aid of another places us at the mercy of that other. European diplomacy is so crooked that it is futile to place faith in the promises of any of them.

I would esteem German friendship as much as British or American or that of the Japanese or the Chinese; I would gratefully accept any help anybody would render in educating and fitting our young men for the coming task, but I would not do anything that would cause useless bloodshed in India. I am not afraid of blood. Blood will have to be shed if we are to gain our freedom. I am not afraid of failures and defeats. Failures and defeats are sometimes the necessary steps to victory. I do not believe in peace at any price; nor pacificism at any cost. I do not believe that "they also serve who only stand and wait." I am for a manly assertion of our rights, even though blood may have to be spilled in asserting or defending them; yet I would consider it highly improper to encourage bloodshed where there is not a ghost of a chance of success. That, in my eyes, is sheer lunacy and I have never made a secret of it. So I protested against my people attempting to stir up revolt in India, under the instigation of a foreign government. It was due to my horror of useless bloodshed. I have no doubt that *agents provocateur* played an important part in instigating those whom your courts have found guilty and sent to the gallows. I believe that the men who have been sacrificed should have lived and worked for the movement for which they have died. So that, in a nutshell, gives you my attitude towards foreign help. Remember, please, sir, that I do not presume to pronounce any judgment on those who think differently and have acted in the light of their consciences. I simply state my opinion and my attitude.

This time the movement has failed. It was bound to fail. But the experience which the Indians engaged in the cause have gained is not lost. Next time, and who knows, the chance may come at no distant date, they will profit by the experience thus gained. The world is not in love with you, sir. There are a dozen peoples in the world who will be glad to see your downfall and help in bringing it about. They will not support the Indian Nationalist and the Indian Revolutionist openly, but they will encourage him in every way they can, without bringing about diplomatic complications. So the Indian will not be altogether friendless when the next opportunity to strike comes. By that time the country also will be better prepared to do something more definite and more spectacular.

Under the circumstances, the question that I wish to put to you is: "Would you do nothing to avert it?" It is in your power to act if you will. The Indians are very easily satisfied. They abhor bloodshed. They do not like revolution. They will gladly remain in the Empire, if permitted to do so on terms of self-respect and honor. Their needs are few. Their life is simple. They care more for spiritual values than for worldly goods. They envy nobody's property. They have no ambition to start on a career of exploitation. All they want is to be let to live and think as they will. At present they are let *to exist*, but not to live. More than 100 million are insufficiently fed. At least 60 millions do not get two meals a day. More than 80% of the boys receive no schooling, and more than 90% of the girls. They work and toil and sweat primarily in the interests of the British capitalist and secondarily in the interests of his Indian colleague. The latter only gets the leavings of the former. The ships, the railways, the leading banking houses, the big insurance offices, the tea plantations, one-half of the cotton mills, about all the woollen mills, most of the paper mills, all jute mills are owned by the former; a few by the latter. The profits of agriculture are divided between your Government and the big landlords. The pressure on land has reduced the size of the ryots' holdings, while the number of mouths requiring food and the number of bodies requiring clothing has increased.

Your Government encourages drinking, speculating and gambling in a way never before conceived. If you have any pity in your heart, sir; if you are a good father and a good husband, I would beseech you to devote but an hour's time to the wages tables printed by your Government in their Report on Prices and Wages (1915). I give a few samples below:

In the district of Patna (Behar), the monthly wage of an able-bodied agricultural laborer in the year 1907 was only R5.62 (say R6) equal to 8s. or $2. In 1873 it was from R3 to R4. Imagine the laborer having a family of four and then conceive how he manages to live on this wage. In Fyzabad (Oude) the monthly wage of an able-bodied agricultural laborer was only R4 (5s. 4d. or $1.33) in 1905, the same as it was in 1873. In 1906 it is given as ranging from R1.87 to R4 a month. From 1873 to 1906 it was never more than R4 a month.

In Cawnpore (U. P.) it was R3.75 in 1873; R3 in 1892; less than 4 in 1896; from 3.44 to R5 in 1898 and from R3.69 to 7 in 1903; at which figure it practically stayed up to 1906, the last year for which figures are given in the report.

In Meerut (U. P.) it was R4.33 in 1906 as against R4.5 in 1873.

In Belgaun (Madras) it was R6.25 in 1912.

In Jubbulpore (C. P.) it was R5 in 1908.

In Raipur (C. P.) it was R5 in 1908.

In Bellary (Madras) it was R4.75 in 1907.

In Salem (Madras) it has never exceeded R3.67 since 1873.

The Government postal runners who carry mails at a trotting pace for several miles a day, often making two trips in 24 hours, are paid the following salaries in the different provinces of your Indian Empire:

Bengal	1913,	R7.75 a month,	$2.58
Behar and Orissa	1913,	6.33 a month,	2.10
United Provinces	1913,	6.25 a month,	2.08
Panjab and N.W.F	1913,	7.75 a month,	2.58
Bombay	1913,	7.5 a month,	2.35
Central Provinces	1913,	7. a month,	2.33
Madras	1913,	7.11 a month,	2.40

(The equivalents in dollars are approximate.)

Postmen who are supposed to be literate, received from R10 to R16 a month (*i. e.*, from $3.33 to $5.33 a month) in the different provinces in 1913.

The scale of wages allowed to unskilled labor in the railway yards of Mirzapore and Cawnpore (U. P.) is given between R5 to R6 per month (*i. e.*, less than $2.00). These are figures of 1914.

In the canal foundry and workshop at Roorkee (U. P.) the daily wage in 1916 was only 4 annas a day (*i. e.*, 8 cents).

In the Cawnpore saddlery establishment, the bullock drivers, the sweepers and the *Bhishties* received only R5 and R6 a month (*i. e.*, less than 8s. or $2.00); the lascars from R6 to R7 (*i. e.*, $2.00 to $2.33).

In the woolen mills in Northern India unskilled labor was paid at R8.12 (*i. e.*, less than $3.00) a month in 1914. These are the rates allowed in big cities. For other big cities the rates may, in some cases, be somewhat better, but in small rural towns and villages, they are considerably less.

Does the Indian laborer, considering his standard of life, the size of his family and the requirements of decency, get a living wage? I am sure that a humane inquirer, not so much interested in the good name of the Government as in truth, will have no hesitation in answering the question in the negative. Any increase in wages has to be divided over the average strength of a family, which will show how disproportionate the increase in wages is to the increase in prices. In a family of five with one or two earning hands the increase in wages is two-fold at the most. While the increase in the cost of living by the increase in prices is five-fold. Your Official Report writers always ignore this important consideration. As for the housing conditions in which Indian workmen live, let me present to you the following testimony from a recent issue of the *Times of India*, Bombay (quoted in the London *Times*, June, 1917):

"It is no unusual sight to find fifteen or twenty persons, of both sexes, lying huddled on the floor of a single room in a stifling atmosphere and a vile stench. A single small window or an open door gives the only ventilation. Furniture there is none, beyond a few brass pots and some pegs. The sanitary arrangements are unspeakable. Every noise and smell that occurs in the neighborhood penetrates the crazy walls and floor and disturbs the sleepers. The chawls are often so rickety that it is a miracle that they do not collapse under their own weight. They seem to be kept up like a house of cards, by the support of their scarcely less rickety neighbors."

As for the Indian laborer getting any education or any leisure for art or for the pursuit of taste, that is out of the question. The condition of the small farmer or *ryot* is even worse. Sir, if you are ever inclined to study the actual conditions of life in India, do not rely upon the "conclusions" of your officers as embodied in reports. Study the facts, given in the reports, but disregard the conclusions. If you seek the aid of an Indian Nationalist he may show you how the reports are drawn up, and how dates and figures have been selected to suit conclusions. Having been a lawyer most of your life you are well aware of the magical properties of special pleading. In the hands of a skillful apologist, the figures can be made to mean anything. Better still, if you want to have a glimpse of conditions of life in India, depute an honest man of the type of Mr. Nevinson to go to Indian villages unaccompanied by officials, and see the things for himself; or to the slums in towns. The slums of Calcutta, Bombay, Madras, Lahore, Delhi, Cawnpore, Lucknow, Benares, will throw the slums of London and New York far back into the shade. The latter are verily a paradise as compared with the former. As to the villages, the less said the better.

The point is in fact conceded by all fair-minded English publicists.

The *Manchester Guardian*, only the other day, discussing the recent increase in the cotton duties, questioned "the wisdom and justice" of this £100,000,000 exaction from India and admitted that "the loss it represents to an extremely poor population like that of India is very much greater than the gain to England." Even the *Morning Post*, that representative of Jingo Imperialism, recognizes the extreme poverty of the masses of India. I will not quote the *Nation* as you do not like that journal. The moneyed classes of India, the Rajas and Maharajas, the bankers and mill owners, the industrial corporations that will fill this loan could not find a more profitable investment. They get 100 per cent. stock for 95 and besides get from 5 to 5½ per cent. interest, in some cases free of income tax for thirty years to come. Upon whom will the burden of interest fall? Neither on the lender nor on the borrower, but mainly on the ryot and the laborer. Do you know, sir, that the average price of salt (wholesale) in Lahore, Punjab, had risen from R1-9-7 a maund in 1912-13 to R2-7-3 in 1916-17? But that in retail sale "the average price of salt per maund (82 lbs.) had risen from R1-14-0 to R5-0-0" (*Tribune*, Lahore, March, 1917). The fresh taxation imposed since the war, which by this loan-cum-gift transaction of 100 million sterling threatens to become permanent, has raised the prices of the necessaries of life to an abnormal extent. The wages remain virtually the same. Your Government which employs large numbers of laboring men in railways, canals, and otherwise have not considered it necessary to raise the wages of the workingmen. Will the private employer do otherwise? I know from personal knowledge how frightfully the poor Indian clerk is sweated in the offices of your Government in India on a mere pittance. Can't you feel for the millions of those little ones whose already scanty, insufficient food is still further reduced by the fresh taxes imposed by your Government to find means to pay the war budget and this permanent addition of £6,000,000 a year to their burden? Don't you know, sir, that in India there are millions of widows (much more than in any other country) who have to support their little ones by their own toil and that every penny of additional taxation hits them hard. The hardships and privations imposed in Europe by the war are nothing as compared with what the Indian masses have been putting up with, for the last fifty years or so. The fiscal policy of your Government has ruined Indian industry. You know it as well as anyone else. Did you notice the letter of Mr. G. W. Forrest in the London *Times* of March 14, 1917, wherein he admitted that "the tale of England's dealing with Indian industry was one of littleness and injustice," and that "by positive prohibition and heavy duties the Indian textile trade in England was destroyed and our own trade was fostered." You and your colleagues have used grandiloquent rhetoric in your defense of the increase in the cotton duties in India and over your concern for India and Indian industries, but you are mistaken if you think that anyone in India is likely to be taken in by your hypocritical professions. Pardon me, sir, I mean no insult when I say "hypocritical professions." The practice is a part of a modern statesman's job. He has to create a certain atmosphere before he can make his people believe that what he does is the only correct thing to do.

Your cotton duties, sir, afford no relief to the Indian poor. It would not have hurt me much, if you had forced or induced the Rajas and the Maharajas, the bankers and the capitalists to contribute even more than 100 million pounds to the war expenses, as it is they who have grown fat, if anyone in India has, under the British regime, but to force the Indian ryot and the Indian wage earner to do it and to continue to pay for it for years to come out of his scanty daily rations is the climax of cruelty. Then the unkindest cut of all is that it should come from you, whom we had associated with feelings of kindness, and pity, for the poor and the workmen.

Your Government has called it a free and spontaneous gift of the people of India! If the members of your cabinet, if the Secretary of State for India, if the Governor General of India and his ministers of the Executive Council, are the people of India, then truly you are right and we wrong. If they are not the people of India, as they are not, then it is a gift by yourself to yourself, of other peoples' money. Again, the statement that the measure was unanimously approved of by the Indian members of the council is a *diplomatic lie*. You know that the matter was settled between your Cabinet as represented by the Secretary of State for India and the Viceroy's Executive Council (which includes only one Indian member nominated by you), before it was announced in the Legislative Council. You know also, sir, and if you don't, you ought to, that the Indian Legislative Council has no power under the law to make any changes in the budget. The budget is entirely beyond their purview. The members can only extol it or criticise it. They can propose resolutions disapproving of some of its provisions which can amount to nothing more than pious wishes even if passed. But the official majority in the Council guarantees the defeat of any hostile resolutions by non-official members. Re this loan-cum-gift transaction, the non-official members of the Legislative Council put a seal on their mouths because they thought it was useless to incur the risk of being called disloyal for a matter which was reported to them as a *fait accompli* and which they could not in any way change or modify; yet two of them did raise a sort of feeble protest.

It is not a Gift by the People of India

The press comments on it, however subdued and timid and halting, leave no doubt about the real mind of India in the matter. The truth has been pointed out by the *Manchester Guardian* and the *Nation*. (Beg your pardon, sir, for mentioning the *Nation* again). The former, in its issue of March 15, remarked: "It is we, who govern India and not the Indian people. The initiative in all financial proposals necessarily comes from the government we appoint in India, and these cannot reach the light of public discussion in the Legislative Council or elsewhere until they have received the sanction of the Secretary of State for India here. For Mr. Chamberlain to throw off upon Indian people the responsibility for originating and devising the 100 million contribution is as unconvincing a rhetorical exercise as the House of Commons has witnessed for many a long day. The responsibility from the first to the last is his and that of the Indian Government. We have said more than once, and we repeat it that in our opinion a wise statesmanship would both find better uses in India for India's millions and employ India more advantageously for the common cause by using more of her manhood and less of her money," I will not quote the *Nation*, sir, which is on this point as explicit, if not more, as the *Manchester Guardian*.

Now, sir, you know that India has been very eager to fight for the Empire. She has supplied you with about 350,000 troops in this war, paying for their services and equipment herself. But 350,000 do not represent even a fraction of her man power, the whole of which she was prepared to throw in this struggle. While Australia and Canada and Ireland have either rejected conscription or are shirking, India has been clamoring for it. You can no longer say that you could not utilize India's manhood because of the prejudice of color. That shibboleth has been shattered by this war and, we hope, for good. The colored people of Asia and Africa are fighting in numbers alongside of the best European troops. Poor people! They believe they are fighting to make the world "safe for democracy!" You cannot say that Indians are lacking in fighting qualities, because the existence of them in a high degree they have proved conclusively in face of difficulties, by no means light and contemptible. That the Indian soldier can hold his own in Europe, even better than the European soldier in Southern Asia, has been established beyond the shadow of a doubt by the experiences of this war. Why, then, won't you use India's manhood and relieve her of this financial exaction which she can ill afford to meet, without suffering egregiously?

India's Teeming Millions want Food and Knowledge of Three R's

The question for India's teeming millions is not "how to live well" but how to live at all. There is no question of comforts for them. What they want, and do not get, is sufficient and nourishing food and a knowledge of the three R's. Your Government is unable to give them the first, and persists in refusing to give them the second; yet when an Indian publicist loses patience and says "slavery has deprived Indians of wealth, honors and freedom, and has reduced them to destitution and starvation," your Viceroy in India cites it as an instance of depraved journalism and a justification for the gagging of the press. He complains that "there are papers in India which magnify the ills from which she suffers" and "which harp upon plague, famine, malaria and poverty" and "ascribe them all to the curse of an alien government." May I ask, sir, if it is not a fact that millions in India die of famine, plague, and malaria? Is it not a fact that the curses and the appalling effects of them, are directly or indirectly traceable to poverty? Many countries on the face of the earth do not grow food sufficient for themselves while India does. Why then should India alone suffer from famines when her food supply, once in a while, falls short of the ordinary year of agricultural "prosperity?" If even during famine years India can supply food to other nations by exports of wheat and other grains, why can't she keep that food at home and feed her own hungry children? Why should plague have stayed in India so long? Why should malaria exact such a heavy annual toll there? The reason is obvious. Because of the ignorance and poverty of the people.

Let us assume that India has not grown poorer under British rule, though there is abundant evidence to the contrary, that the masses have become poorer and are becoming poorer every day; let us also assume that in the matter of education India was worse off under native rule—*i. e.*, before the introduction of the British rule—a period of history when no other part of the world was any the better. Is it not a matter of shame, that after 150 years of British rule, when most of the other national governments in other parts of the world have reduced their illiteracy almost to zero point, India should still have more than 90% of its population illiterate. Is it not a matter of shame, that of all the grain producing countries of the world India alone should be so miserably situated as to be unable to supply sufficient and nourishing food to her sons and daughters. Don't you think, sir, that the Indians have reason to feel sore when they see that the food grown by them is denied to them; that it is almost snatched from their mouths; that others should eat the food which is grown by them, that even in the best of years millions of them must be contented with only one meal a day, and that of the coarsest grain.

Do you remember, Mr. Lloyd George, how bitter you felt against the capitalist, when you yourself in your boyhood, felt the pinch of want? Have you forgotten all that you said in the Lime-house speech? I repeat that the sufferings of the British laborer and workingmen, the trials of the

British poor are nothing compared with those of the Indian ryot and the Indian workingmen and the Indian clerks in your employ in that country. Yet you have no feeling to spare for them, and those that have, you and your Government brand as malcontents and seditionists. Don't you think, sir, that the Indian ryot and the Indian poor are being crushed under the weight of two capitalisms superimposed upon each other—one foreign and the other indigenous? When we ask for freedom to manage our own affairs you say we are not fit to do so. But what can we do to ourselves which will be worse than what you have done us? If left free, we might bring to book the indigenous capitalists whom, in the interests of your own capitalists, you have been supporting and fattening. But even if we fail to do so, we shall at any rate have upon us the burden of only a single weight. Your colleagues say that in refusing self-government to India they are actuated by devotion to India; that they do not want to hand over the millions of India to the tender mercies of a small minority of educated and wealthy men in whose hands the government will inevitably drift. Supposing it does, it will be easy for the masses to keep the minority in check. They can revolt and rebel, but under your Government the bureaucracy is all powerful. The truth is, sir, that the condition of these very millions, in whose interests, you say, you are reluctant to give power to the educated and the wealthy few, is a standing condemnation of your government there. The educated minority and the wealthy few are fairly well off under your regime. It is the ignorant ryot and the millions of workingmen and women who suffer. In the words of one of your distinguished writers (W. Lily), they do not live but just exist.

Recently the *Times* said that the British were "the trustees of the welfare of India's millions." Who are these millions for whom you are trustees? Are they those homeless, educationless millions who get only one meal a day or are they those who have benefitted from your schools and are wealthy? If the former, you have failed in your trust. If the latter, they are quite fit to manage their own affairs. It was only the other day that Mr. Austen Chamberlain was reported to have said (*Times*, London, March 30) at a luncheon given to him and the India's so-called representatives at the Imperial conference (one of whom was a Lieutenant Governor interested in extending India's sphere of subjection) that "India will not remain and ought not to remain content to be a hewer of wood and a drawer of water for the rest of the Empire." Noble words these, full of hope and encouragement. But what a sad and a crushing acknowledgment of the present helpless condition of India. It is a truthful statement for which the Indians ought to be grateful to Mr. Chamberlain. At the present moment India is a mere "hewer of wood and a drawer of water" for the rest of the Empire. Against that her sons protest, and will continue to protest, as long as the wrongs of the country are not redressed, your press act, your sedition laws, jails and prisons notwithstanding.

The position, Mr. Lloyd George, is pathetic. When we ask for more outlay on education, you say, no, the condition of the finances will not permit of that. When we point out the way to find finances, you say, "no, further taxes are impossible and retrenchment in public expenditure in other departments undesirable." When we say, "give us the management and we will do it," you say, "no you are unfit." The result is that you will neither educate the masses yourself nor will you let us educate them. Yet you hold their ignorance a valid ground for refusing us our right to manage our own affairs. When, however, you want money for Imperial purposes you raise loans, impose taxes, and reduce public expenditure on education and public works. You have done this not only now, for the purposes of this bloody war, but you have done so in the past in building railways for your merchants and to fight your wars in Africa, in China, in Afghanistan, in fact, all over the old world. It is true the present is a trying time for you and you may have a pretence of justification in this crisis in your Imperial life. But so long as you refuse the conscription of wealth in your home islands, what right have you to impose this conscription of India's money resources? You have not forced the dominions to make monetary contributions. In fact you have advanced them over £140,000,000 from your own funds. You have not so far called upon the British capitalists to pay even a fraction of their wealth. You have simply taxed their excessive profits. Why should you have made an exception in the case of India? India is the poorest part of the

Empire. Yet it is she who has been selected for this exceptional treatment. She had already made lavish gifts of money and provisions and equipment. Her gifts were in entire disproportion to her means. Compared with your dominions' resources and their money sacrifices India's contribution stood higher than those of the former. Yet you selected India for this compulsory money contribution because India is the only part of the Empire which you could thus treat. India is the only part of the Empire which has been forced to give $500,000,000 as a *free gift*. Even the fabulously rich United States which have made huge war profits from you and your other allies have not thought of a national gift. Yet imperial sophistry represented by your imperial publicists and officials, represents that Great Britain exacts no tribute from India and makes no profit out of her connection with India and that she rules India simply out of philanthropic and humanitarian motives.

Waste

One would have thought that under the pressure of the war, your Government in India would make an honest and earnest effort to reduce expenditure on public services, at least under heads mainly ornamental or which only afford luxuries to your agents in India; but on the other hand, what is the actual situation? A perusal of the proceedings of the Imperial Legislative Council and also of the Provincial Councils shows that all efforts made by the non-official members to obtain additional money for education and sanitation by the reduction of expenditure on luxuries, were opposed by your Government, and were consequently defeated. All efforts to reduce expenditure on comforts were of course resisted by those who enjoyed them, and it is they whose votes count in the Indian Councils. For example, it was proposed that the huge expenditure incurred by the different Government Departments, Imperial and Provincial, in moving to the Hills for seven months of the year, should be reduced, at least partially. Many persons competent to express an opinion on the subject, among them Lord

Carmichael, the retiring Governor of Bengal, have placed it on record that this "exodus to the hills" was not necessary, and was in fact prejudicial to the interests of good government; yet the Government opposed the motion of the non-official member and he was forced to withdraw it. A similar motion to curtail the expenditure on the ornamentation of the residence of the Lieutenant Governor of the United Provinces was also opposed and met a similar fate. The huge allowances made to the heads of the different governments in India for kitchen expenses, for dispensing hospitality, and for traveling in royal style have not been reduced by a penny. The Punjab Government has provided in its current budget a large amount of money for providing palatial residences for its officers in summer resorts, and has sanctioned large pensions, from father to son, for a few of their Indian supporters. These men are mostly wealthy men. They did nothing more than help you in your suppressive and exploiting policy. Your Government naturally rewards them. Is it not bribery. If an expert financier were to examine into these items, which can only pass unchallenged in a country wherein the people have no voice in the raising of the taxes and in spending them, it would be found that great savings could be effected and the money thus made available used for other urgent needs of the people. The fact is that the Indian ryot who pays for all these extravagances has no voice to check the vagaries of those who spend his money for their own comforts. I have not mentioned the lavish scale on which special traveling allowances are granted to high officials in India. It is a matter of common knowledge that these officials do not spend as much as they draw under this head. Yet it is actually proposed that the salaries and the allowances for the European members of the Indian services be substantially raised. *Verily, taxation without representation* is a crime of the worst possible kind.

Democracy

Mr. Lloyd George, you and your colleagues in the Government of Great Britain, say that in fighting the Germans you are fighting the battle of Democracy, to make the world safe from autocracy and militarism, that you are fighting for rights of small nations, and for the domination of right over might. The United States has joined the war for the same reason. I have seen numerous recruiting posters exhibited in New York City exhorting young Americans to enlist in the army "to make the world safe" for Democracy. I have not the slightest doubt of the sincerity of the American professions because their international record is so far clean. Vide their record in Cuba and the Philippines. Can we say the same for Great Britain? I am afraid not, so long at least, as you continue to deny self-government to India, the second of the two biggest democracies of the world. Here is a nation of 315 million human beings (or say several nations, if you wish, as your publicists are so fond of repeating *ad nauseam* that India is not a nation) whom you are governing by the force of might, without their consent, and on absolutely despotic lines; whom you deny freedom of speech, freedom of association and freedom of education; whom you tax without their consent and then spend those taxes outside of their country, and in providing luxuries to your representatives in India or in bribing such Indians as uphold you in your possessions. I have no doubt that you are sincere in your denunciation of German militarism. For myself I have no use for Czars and Kaisers, Emperors and Sultans, and I dare say that you, too, have none. Thus I am in full sympathy with your efforts to exterminate the race of Kaisers. So far you are right. But an Indian cannot help smiling rather cynically when he hears you saying that you are waging the war to make the world safe for democracy. Your conduct in India and in Egypt, and in Persia belies your protestations.

As to Small Nations

In defending your conduct you urge that India is not a nation. Very well, sir, divide India into small nations and give them self-government separately. You will admit that there are parts of India which are homogenous, entitled to be called small nations in the sense in which Belgium, Switzerland, Denmark, and Holland are. The bulk of the population follow the same religion, speak the same language and belong to the same race. Remember, please, that I do not admit that India is not a nation or that the sameness of language, religion and race is necessary for a political national existence. Switzerland, Canada, the United States, South Africa, Russia, and Austria-Hungary have demolished that theory.

The apologists of the present system of Government in India say that the Indian people are not sufficiently educated in the principles and practice of politics and that their ignorance and illiteracy make it necessary for the British to continue to rule them from without, until they are fit to establish and maintain a democratic form of government. I have already made some remarks about illiteracy and shown that the responsibility for it rests on your shoulders. If you, sir, are to be the sole judge of the educational requirements of the Indian people, their progress is bound to hang on your convenience. No one in possession is anxious to be dispossessed and if the time and method of his dispossession is to be determined by himself, then woe to the dispossessed! But, sir, you forget that literacy is not education. The Indian masses have a background of centuries of culture which places them in the matter of intelligence and character, in a better position than even the literate millions of European and American countries. And after all, it is intelligence and culture that count most in the fixing of final values.

As for their training in political life, how are they to get it, if you make it a penal offence for their leaders to tell them that the present system of Government is unnatural, harmful, and a hindrance to progress? The masses cannot grasp principles unless one illustrates these principles by their application to the affairs of every day life. Your Government and your courts say that an agitation for home rule is legal and permissible, but any criticism that is likely to create dissatisfaction is illegal and deserves to be suppressed high-handedly. You know from experience, sir, that the masses require to be led. No government is willing to make changes unless compelled from below. That is as true of democratic America as of monarchical England. Much more must it be so in the case of countries under foreign yoke. To carry the people with them, the leaders must expose the existing evils and stress the necessity and urgency of sweeping changes in political conditions. The moment they proceed to do so with any degree of effectiveness, they are charged with an attempt to create disaffection and convicted of sedition. Do you honestly believe that any people on the face of the earth can make any progress in political education when they are ruled by a Press Act which stops criticism and discussion in the following terms:

Section of the Indian Press Act of 1910

Whenever it appears to the Local Government that any printing press in respect of which any security has been deposited as required by Section 3 is used for the purpose of printing or publishing any newspaper, book, or other document containing any words, signs or visible representations which are likely to have a tendency directly, or indirectly, whether by inference, suggestion, allusion, metaphor, implication or otherwise:

(a) To incite to murder or to any offense under the Explosives Substances Act of 1908, or to any act of violence or

(b) To seduce any officer, soldier, or sailor in the Army or Navy of His Majesty from his allegiance or his duty or

(c) To bring into hatred or contempt His Majesty or the Government established by the law in British India, or the Administration of Justice in British India or any native Prince or Chief under the suzeranity of His Majesty or any class or section of His Majesty's subjects in British India or to excite disaffection towards His Majesty or the said Government or any such Prince or Chief or

(d) To put any person in fear or to cause any annoyance to him and thereby induce him to deliver to any person any property or valuable security, or to do any act which he is not legally bound to do or to omit any act which he is legally entitled to do or

(e) To encourage or incite any person to interfere with the administration of the law or with the maintenance of law and order or

(f) To convey any threat of injury to a public servant, or to any person in whom the public servant is believed to be interested, with a view to inducing that person to do any act or to forbear to do any act connected with the exercise of his public functions the Local Government may, by notice in writing to the keeper of such printing press, stating or describing the words, signs or visible representations which in its opinion are of the nature described above, declare the security deposited in respect of such Press and all copies of such newspaper, book, or other document wherever found to be forfeited to His Majesty.

EXPLANATION I: In clause c the expression disaffection includes disloyalty and all feelings of enmity.

EXPLANATION II: Comments expressing the disapproval of the measures of the Government of any such native Prince or Chief as aforesaid with a view to obtain their alteration by lawful means or of the administration or other action of the Government or any such native Prince or Chief or of the administration of Justice in British India without exciting or attempting to excite hatred, contempt, or disaffection, do not come under the scope of clause c.

Can any people make headway in the art of self-government who are governed by a foreign bureaucracy aided by an army of Indian Czars regulating the very minutest details of their life? You know that this over government of India is a direct result of your rule. Before you came the Indian village was a self-governed unit. (See statements of Monroe, Elphinstone, Metcalfe, and Lawrence.) Even now the people in the Native States are in this respect better off than the people of British India. The Education Minister of your Cabinet, Mr. H. A. L. Fisher has, after a visit to India, placed it on record that "the inhabitants of a well governed Native State are, on the whole, happier and more contented than the inhabitants of British India. They are more lightly taxed; the pace of the administration is less urgent and exacting. They feel that they do things for themselves instead of having everything done by a cold and alien benevolence." Yet if an Indian leader were to point this out and ask the Indian masses to improve their lot by demanding and winning for themselves the right to manage their own affairs, and by driving out those influences that stand in their way, he would be persecuted and imprisoned or transported.

The first axiom for political progress is that the people should throw away their attitude of submission to oppression, tyranny, high-handedness, and conditions of slavery whether imposed by a national or a foreign Government. They have a right to revolt if they have the means to do so successfully. But in any case, they have a right to discuss, agitate and organize for changes. This they cannot do unless they have a free press, a free platform, and the right of free association. In India the first is denied by the Press Act, the second by the comprehensive sections of the Penal Code, and the third by the so-called "Seditious Meetings Act." What little was left has been done away with under the extensive powers taken and exercised by the Executive under the plea of war exigency by the "Defense of India Act." While every other part of the Empire, including the "Mother Country" is discussing political and economic changes of an extremely radical character, such as the establishment of a more effective Imperial Parliament and Preferential Tariffs after the war, not to speak of constructive programmes for education, and industrial rejuvenation, the Indian leaders are "officially" advised to be mum, and any effort to rouse the country to a consciousness of its rights and duties is characterized as perverted, ill-timed, and inconsistent with loyalty.

The advocates of "Home Rule" are being openly hampered in their propaganda. Papers advocating home rule have been persecuted, and leaders have been prohibited from entering provincial areas. But what is worse is that the Criminal Investigation Department have been instructed to take down the names of all those who have enlisted in the cause, either as active or passive workers. A deputation of representatives of the press that waited on the Viceroy to lay their grievances before him has been lectured on the impropriety of thus raising the question at this juncture and has otherwise been treated with shocking discourtesy.

In conclusion, let me ask you, sir, to notice the coercive methods by which the War Loan is being raised in India. Poor underpaid subordinate officials are being forced to purchase Government stock. They will surely purchase the stock and win the good-will of their officers, but just as surely they will squeeze the cost out of the people. That will be strictly in accord with the standards of loyalty set up by your officials!

Mr. David Lloyd George, I have addressed this letter to you, because at this moment you seem to be the only British statesman possessed of imagination. Exercise your imagination, sir, a little and save India for the Empire; win the gratitude and blessings of a fifth of the human race—of a people who were one of the first pioneers of civilization in the world, who laid the foundations of culture, which you profess to be so very anxious to save. Remember that the Indians were rich, prosperous, free, self-governing, civilized and great, both in peace and war, when not only Britain but even "Greece and Rome were nursing the tenants of the wilderness." The Indians have lost their freedom because they oppressed the people under them and as surely as night follows day, the British will lose all that makes them great to-day, if they continue to oppress and exploit the subject races within their Empire. The world cannot be safe for democracy unless India is self-governed. Nor can there be any lasting peace in the world, so long as India and China are not strong enough to protect themselves.

Pardon me, sir, if I have disturbed you at such a critical moment; though it is folly to presume that you could be disturbed in the slightest degree by such a letter. I have written it out of a sense of duty as sacred as that which inspires you in your herculean task; and if you are inclined to think harshly of me for this letter, just try to put yourself in my position and decide what then would be your point of view.

LAJPAT RAI.

New York City, June 13, 1917.